MW00899227

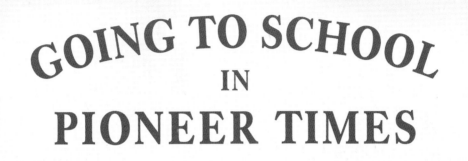

GOING TO SCHOOL
IN
PIONEER TIMES

by Kerry A. Graves

Consultant: Anita Sue Clement, Education Specialist
Stuhr Museum of the Prairie Pioneer

Blue Earth Books

an imprint of Capstone Press
Mankato, Minnesota

Blue Earth Books are published by Capstone Press
151 Good Counsel Drive, P.O. Box 669, Mankato, Minnesota 56002
http://www.capstone-press.com

Library of Congress Cataloging-in-Publication Data
Graves, Kerry A.
   Going to school in pioneer times / by Kerry A. Graves.
   p. cm.—(Going to school in history)
   Includes bibliographical references (p.31) and index.
   ISBN 0-7368-0804-3
   1. Rural education—Middle West—History—Juvenile literature. 2. Education—Middle West—History—Juvenile literature. [1. Frontier and pioneer life. 2. Schools—History.] I. Title. II. Series.
   LC5147.M55 G72 2002
   370'.977—dc21
                                                                                    00-011623

Summary: Discusses the school life of children in pioneer times, including lessons, books, teachers, examinations, and special days.
Includes activities and sidebars.

Editorial Credits

Editor: Rachel Koestler
Designer and Illustrator: Heather Kindseth
Product Planning Editor: Lois Wallentine
Photo Researcher: Heidi Schoof

1 2 3 4 5 6 07 06 05 04 03 02

Photo Credits

State Historical Society of Wisconsin, cover, 12, 18; State Historical Society of Iowa, 14–15; Mary Keithan, 8, 17; Brown County Historical Society, 24; Fred Hultstrand History in Pictures Collection, NDIRS-NDSU, Fargo, 3 (top), 9 (top), 11, 15 (right), 23, 27; James E. Byrne, 3 (bottom), 9 (bottom), 14 (left); Capstone Press/Gary Sundermeyer, 29; Courtesy of AA Forbes Collection, Western History Collection, University of Oklahoma Library, 5 (both); Archive Photos, 7; Underwood and Underwood/F. G. Weller (private collection) 19; The Newberry Library/Stock Montage, Inc., 21 (top); Library of Congress, 21 (bottom); Photo by St. Paul Dispatch-Pioneer Press, Minnesota Historical Society, 22; Minnesota Historical Society, 25; Courtesty of Anita Sue Clement (private collection), 28

Contents

A New Home in the West

In the mid-1800s, people from the eastern states began settling the western territories of the United States. Many pioneer families left the crowded eastern states and moved west in hope of a better life. Some of these pioneers traveled to the modern-day states of Illinois, Wisconsin, Iowa, Minnesota, Nebraska, South Dakota, and North Dakota. They packed their belongings in covered wagons and hitched oxen, mules, or horses to the wagons to pull the load. Pioneers journeyed for several months across hundreds of miles (kilometers) of unsettled land.

The U.S. government gave pioneers a piece of land. When pioneers arrived at this land claim, they had to build a home and farm buildings. Some families lived in their wagons or in tents until a permanent shelter could be built. In wooded areas, pioneers cut down trees to build log homes. Nails were expensive and hard to find in pioneer times. Pioneer men cut notches in the logs to fit them together, then filled gaps between the logs with a mud and grass mixture called chinking.

On the prairie, where forests were scarce, pioneers built "soddys." They used a special plow to cut strips of dirt and grass from the prairie, each about 4 inches (10 centimeters) thick. They then cut the sod into blocks about 1 foot (30 centimeters) wide and 3 feet (91 centimeters) long. Pioneers stacked sod blocks on top of each other to build walls.

In some areas of the prairie, pioneers dug their homes into the side of a hill. They stacked sod bricks in front of the dugout to make a wall that sealed the hole. Some families plastered the insides of soddys and dugouts with a homemade mixture of lime, sand, mud, and horsehair or grass. Plastered walls sometimes kept mice, snakes, and insects from digging through the walls. Pioneers covered window openings with blankets or animal hides to prevent cold winds and dust from blowing into their homes.

Few towns existed on the western frontier during the early 1800s. Most supplies had to be made by hand rather than purchased at shops. Pioneers crafted their own furniture, clothes, butter, candles, and soap.

In the 1860s, the transcontinental railroad was finished, and many pioneers rushed to build homes in the Midwest. As frontier settlements grew, towns were formed. People opened general stores, bakeries, post offices, lumber mills, and schools. After businesses opened, pioneers bought many supplies from stores.

Prairie pioneers built sod houses (above). Some pioneers called sod-cutting plows "grasshoppers" because the plows' rods resembled insect wings (below).

5

Map of the Western Frontier, late 1800s

Washington Territory

Montana Territory

Missouri River

Dakota Territory

Minnesota

Oregon

Idaho Territory

Wyoming Territory

Wisconsin

Michigan

California

transcontinental railroad

Nebraska

Iowa

Illinois

Nevada

Utah Territory

Colorado Territory

Kansas

Missouri

Arizona Territory

New Mexico Territory

unorganized territory

Texas

6

The Frontier

In the 1800s, pioneers called unsettled territories of the western United States the frontier. The frontier stretched from the Missouri River to the California coast. The U.S. government divided the frontier into territories. Upper midwestern states also were part of the frontier.

The U.S. government passed laws to encourage people to move to new territories. In 1844, Congress passed the Townsite Act. This law allowed pioneers to buy 320 acres (130 hectares) of land for $1.25 per acre. Later, the government offered veterans of the Mexican War (1846–1848) and the Civil War (1861–1865) free land in honor of their military service. The Homestead Act of 1862 gave 160 acres (65 hectares) of free land to pioneers who were interested in building homes and farms west of the Missouri River. Thousands of pioneers traveled in wagon trains across the plains, prairies, and mountains to help settle the West.

Pioneers built schoolhouses in a central location. Some schools were located in town. Others were in a rural area.

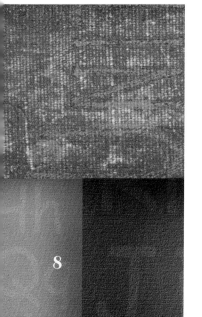

Farming the land was difficult. Pioneers spent long hours plowing, planting, and harvesting crops. Farmers used crude plows called sodbusters to break the soil for planting. Early pioneers also earned the nickname "sodbusters" because they used an ax to break the sod for planting the first corn crop.

Pioneers suffered through many hardships. Temperatures could reach more than 100°F (38°C) during summer and drop below 0°F (minus 18°C) during winter. Droughts, heavy rains, hail, or an early frost sometimes damaged crops. On the prairie, strong winds blew clouds of dust into the air, blinding farmers who were trying to work in the fields. During blizzards, snow blew so thickly that pioneers sometimes tied ropes between the house and the barn so they could find their way to the animals and back to the house.

Families worked together to farm the land. Each family member had assigned chores to finish every day. Women and girls started cooking fires in the early-morning hours while men and boys gathered their tools and hitched the oxen to plows. Some pioneer children went to school during the day and finished their chores when they returned home. Pioneer women spent the day baking, sewing, and washing laundry. Many women and girls also helped with planting and harvesting. In addition, pioneer children often helped their parents feed the farm animals, milk the cows, gather eggs, churn butter, and weed the garden.

On the prairie frontier, children attended school in sod schoolhouses (above). Pioneer schoolhouses did not have indoor plumbing. Children used outhouses, or privies (below).

9

Schooling on the Western Frontier

The main goal of frontier schools was to teach children to read and write. Most parents wanted their children to be able to read the Bible. Some pioneer families wanted their children to learn arithmetic. These families often operated businesses in pioneer towns. Immigrant families relied on schools to teach their children English.

Most pioneer schools held classes from mid-November to April, after the fall harvest and before the spring planting. But the schoolhouse was open whenever a teacher could be found. For some towns, this meant holding school sessions during summer. Some students took summer classes but only attended when class did not interfere with farm chores. Younger children often took summer classes because they could not help with as many chores. Many children quit school after they learned to read.

The pioneer community supported the schoolteacher. Parents paid tuition for each child. These fees averaged $1 to $3 per student. Tuition rates varied, depending on how long the child stayed in school and what subjects he or she studied. Some children did chores at the school in exchange for lessons.

Most pioneer schools taught students who ranged in age from 4 to 21. Schoolchildren of all ages often studied in a single classroom. Class sizes varied depending on the season and number of families in the area.

Most pioneer schools did not have specific grades like schools in the eastern cities.

Children progressed through different levels of readers, spellers, and arithmetic as fast as they could, depending on how often they could attend. Once they mastered a subject, children advanced to more difficult subjects. Older children sometimes helped teach the younger children.

Students in frontier schools often worked independently. The teacher met with small groups of students throughout the day. Teachers expected the rest of the students to study quietly when it was not their group's turn.

Early frontier schools did not have writing paper. Most schools could not afford paper and ink supplies. Students wrote arithmetic problems and spelling words on slates. Instead of pens, students used slate pencils or chalk. After the teacher reviewed the assignment, children erased their work with a damp cloth. They sometimes used an eraser made from a wooden block covered with sheepskin.

In this late 1800s photo, students pose with their books and writing slates.

Make a Writing Slate

What You Need

thin piece of plywood or craft wood, cut 8 inches by
  12 inches (20 centimeters by 30 centimeters)
sandpaper
cloth rag
masking tape, 1 inch (2.5 centimeters) wide

newspapers
blackboard-finish spray paint
white or colored chalk
felt eraser

What You Do

1. Use the sandpaper to sand all the edges of the wooden board until it is smooth. Be careful of splinters. Lightly sand the top and bottom of the board.

2. Wipe all surfaces of the board with the rag to remove any loose sawdust.

3. Place strips of masking tape in a border along the outside edges of the board. Make sure the edge of the masking tape is flush with the edge of the board so the tape does not fold over the edge.

4. Spread out two to three layers of newspaper on a firm surface. Place the board with the taped side up in the center of the paper.

5. Following the directions on the paint can, lightly spray the surface of the wood. Allow it to dry completely, then apply a second coat. If paint appears thin in spots, spray additional coats. After each coat, allow paint to dry completely.

6. Remove the masking tape from your slate.

7. Use white or colored chalk to write on your slate. Erase your work with the felt eraser.

13

Pioneer Schoolteachers

Many teachers in the early 1800s had limited training as educators. Most teachers were young men or women who had completed a full course of schooling and had an interest in teaching school. The teacher often was only 16 or 17 years old. Some teachers traveled from the East to take teaching jobs on the frontier.

By the late 1800s, farms and towns were firmly established. Children had more time for school, and parents wanted teachers to have more training. By 1860, 11 normal schools had opened on the East Coast. These schools offered a two-year training program for teachers. Some teachers took normal training at local high schools.

Some communities did not have a qualified teacher. Convincing teachers to travel to frontier towns was difficult, especially since most pioneer communities could not afford to pay schoolteachers much money. Many teachers made only $10 to $35 a month. Some schools remained closed for several years after a teacher left. If a town could not find a teacher, children studied at home with their parents.

Some teachers found rooms to rent at boarding houses. These rooms cost $2 to $3 a week. Many teachers had to "board around" with the

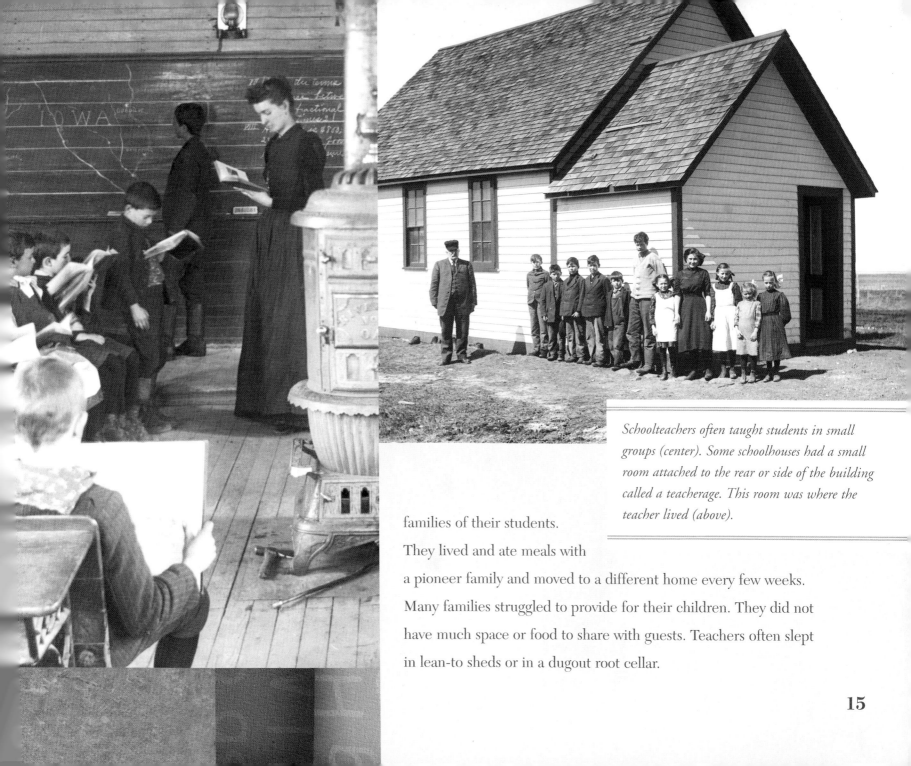

Schoolteachers often taught students in small groups (center). Some schoolhouses had a small room attached to the rear or side of the building called a teacherage. This room was where the teacher lived (above).

families of their students. They lived and ate meals with a pioneer family and moved to a different home every few weeks. Many families struggled to provide for their children. They did not have much space or food to share with guests. Teachers often slept in lean-to sheds or in a dugout root cellar.

The One-room Schoolhouse

Because many pioneer farms were scattered across the prairie, pioneers built the schoolhouse in a central location. Some schoolhouses were made from sod. In some areas, each family donated an amount of wood to use in building the school. Everyone helped "raise" the school. This building event brought members of a pioneer community together.

Schoolhouses had many functions. In many pioneer towns, the schoolhouse also was the church. Teachers used the schoolhouse for recitals and examinations. In some areas, one building served as a school during the week, a church on Sunday, and a place for community meetings.

The schoolhouse usually was a large rectangular building with windows along the sides. Some schools had a small entryway for hanging coats and hats. In most schoolhouses, one or more blackboards covered the wall behind the teacher's desk. Most schoolhouses had a space above the blackboard for hanging writing examples or artwork. The teacher's desk sometimes was set on a raised platform so the teacher had a good view of the room.

Seating arrangements varied from school to school. In some schools, desks lined the side walls. Students often sat on long benches at the desks. Other schools had

Rules for The School
Boys - no hats
1. Come into the schoolroom quietly
2. Take your seats at once
3. Always raise your hand to speak
4. No whispering or talking to others
5. No pulling braids or poking
6. No carving on the desk

Cleaning
Mon. Mary
Tues. Susan
Wed. Laura
Thurs. Grace
Fri. Sarah

Firewood
Mon. John
Tues. Jacob
Wed. Sally
Thurs. Martha
Fri. Joseph

Pioneer students often sat at double desks. Two children sat together and shared each desk.

rows of student benches or individual desks that faced the teacher. The youngest children sat in the front desks, and the older students sat at the back of the classroom. Many pioneer schoolteachers separated the boys and the girls. Girls sat on one side of the room, and boys sat on the opposite side.

In the mid-1800s, indoor plumbing did not exist. Children used outhouses, or privies, behind the schoolhouse. Next to the front or rear entrance, the teacher kept a water bucket. Thirsty children used a dipper to scoop water from the bucket. Some schoolhouses had a well nearby from which to draw water. If the schoolhouse did not have a well, children often took turns filling the water bucket at a nearby stream.

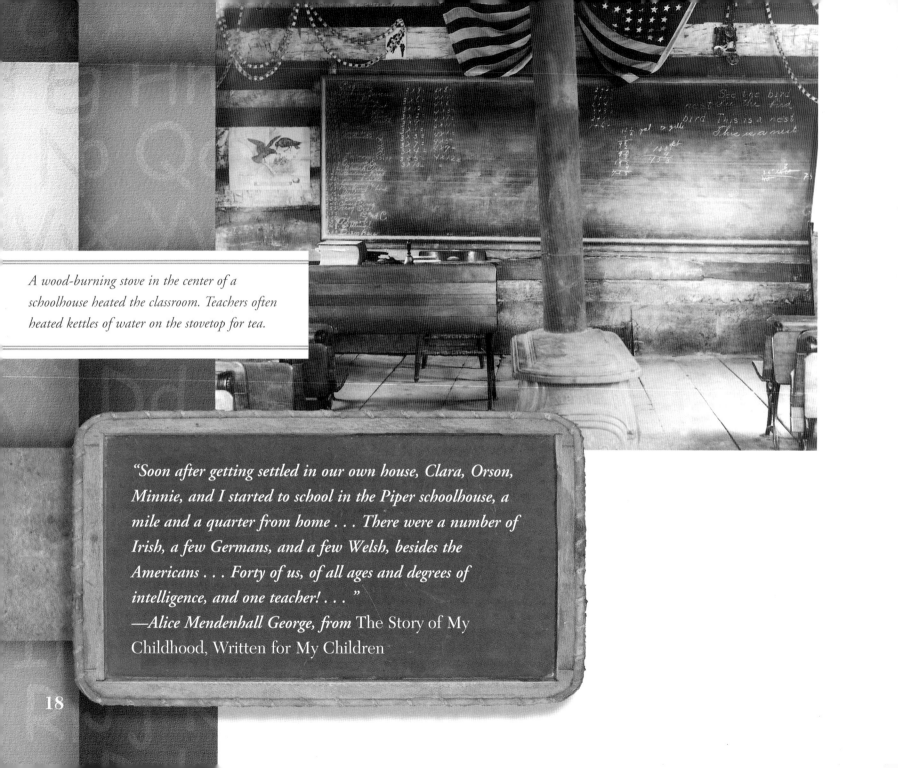

A wood-burning stove in the center of a schoolhouse heated the classroom. Teachers often heated kettles of water on the stovetop for tea.

"Soon after getting settled in our own house, Clara, Orson, Minnie, and I started to school in the Piper schoolhouse, a mile and a quarter from home . . . There were a number of Irish, a few Germans, and a few Welsh, besides the Americans . . . Forty of us, of all ages and degrees of intelligence, and one teacher! . . . "
—Alice Mendenhall George, from The Story of My Childhood, Written for My Children

Keeping Order in the Schoolhouse

In the 1800s, teachers were expected to teach good morals to their students. They punished students for tardiness, speaking out of turn, falling asleep during class, whispering, pulling pranks, fighting, or causing other disruptions. A Nebraska newspaper in the 1880s advertised a teaching position by requesting a "man teacher, as good at lickin' as at learnin'."

Schoolteachers sometimes were strict. Many teachers hit unruly students with a ruler or a small tree branch called a switch. They sometimes locked the child in a closet. Other teachers embarrassed students to punish them. In some schools, students who did not learn their lessons wore a dunce cap. This tall, pointed cap drew attention to the student. Some teachers also made the student wearing the dunce cap sit on a stool in front of the class.

Students sometimes pulled pranks on other students during class.

School Days

The school day started at sunrise. During fall and winter, the schoolteacher started a fire in the stove early each morning to warm the room. At eight o'clock, the teacher stood in the schoolhouse doorway and rang a hand bell, calling the children to class. As the students entered the building, they "made their manners" to the teacher. This morning greeting sometimes was followed by a bow from the boys and a curtsy from the girls.

Teachers on the frontier designed school lessons to give children a basic education in a variety of subjects. Most pioneer schools taught reading, writing, and arithmetic. Students also learned religion, penmanship, composition, grammar, spelling, and geography. Many schools offered music, drawing, and singing lessons. A few frontier schoolteachers taught lessons in botany and philosophy.

Schoolbooks were expensive, and some schools did not have enough for all the students. Many schoolteachers taught lessons from personal books or required students to bring a Bible from home. Most pioneer children studied from *McGuffey's Eclectic Readers* by William Holmes. This series of textbooks offered lessons for different grade levels. The *First Reader* was a primer. Primers taught young children

to read through simple rhymes. Primer books also included lessons in the alphabet, spelling, and numbers. The *Second Reader* through the *Sixth Reader* included stories, famous speeches, and poems. These works taught students good morals by promoting hard work, honesty, charity, and proper manners.

Readers also taught children proper penmanship. Students copied letters from their primers onto their slates. Some students practiced penmanship by writing essays in composition books.

In pioneer schools, all children wrote with their right hand. If students tried writing with their left hand, the teacher forced them to switch to their right hand. Some teachers tied students' left arm behind their back to keep them from writing with their left hand.

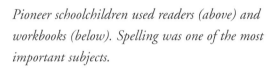

Pioneer schoolchildren used readers (above) and workbooks (below). Spelling was one of the most important subjects.

Some students sang their multiplication tables to the tune of "Yankee Doodle." This photo of an arithmetic activity was taken in the early 1900s.

Math Buzz

Number games such as Math Buzz strengthened students' multiplication skills. Schoolchildren sat in a circle and chose a buzz number. Each student began to count in turn. Whenever a student reached a multiple of the base number, the student said "buzz" instead of a number. For example, for the number three, the buzz count would be one, two, buzz, four, five, buzz, seven, eight, buzz . . . You can play Math Buzz with your friends. Choose different numbers to improve your multiplication skills.

Arithmetic drills improved students' problem-solving speed. The schoolteacher wrote an arithmetic problem on the blackboard while the students solved it on their slates. Many teachers also expected students to solve difficult problems in their heads. This exercise was called oral arithmetic. Teachers sometimes said a problem out loud and asked a student to answer it. Pioneer students also memorized addition and multiplication tables.

Most frontier schools took breaks from classes throughout the day. Students took a lunch break over the noon hour. Most students brought lunches from home in metal or wooden buckets. After lunch, students went outdoors for fresh air and exercise. Even in cold weather, most students were eager to get out of the classroom to play. Teachers also called a short recess in the morning and another in the afternoon. These breaks allowed children to use the privies or to drink a dipper of water.

Pioneer children played "In and Out the Window" during recess. Children sang a song while the child who was "it" weaved between the children in the circle. At the end of the song, whomever "it" was standing beside became "it" for the next time.

Some schoolchildren played baseball during recess. When recess was over, the schoolteacher rang the bell, calling the students back to class.

During recess, most children played group games such as tag, hide-and-seek, and baseball. They also played Fox and Geese in the snow. Using their feet and legs, they cleared paths in the snow in the shape of a spoked wheel. They then chose one child to be the fox. The fox tried to tag the rest of the children, who were geese. The players had to stay within the paths of the wheel.

Girls had many of their own games. They often jumped rope. Many girls played games such as Cat's Cradle with long pieces of string tied together at the ends. They wove the string between their fingers to make shapes and designs. Some girls played hopscotch or braided flower chains. Girls made daisy-chain crowns for their hair by weaving together the flower stems.

Play Marbles

During recess, many pioneer children played with clay marbles. You can play a simple version of marbles with your friends. Before playing marbles, decide whether or not you will play "for keeps." If you play for keeps, you keep the marbles you knock from the ring. If you do not play for keeps, you return the marbles to their owners at the end of the game.

What You Need

two or more players

flat, smooth area of ground, about 10 feet (3 meters) across

tape measure or yard stick

chalk

a large shooter marble for each player, about $^3/_4$ inch (1.9 centimeters) in diameter

4 to 6 smaller target marbles, about $^1/_2$ inch (1.3 centimeters) in diameter

What You Do

1. Draw a circle that is 7 feet (2 meters) across in the center of the playing area.
2. Each player places an equal number of target marbles in the center of the circle. You can decide on the number of marbles. The more marbles played by each player, the longer the game will last.
3. Decide who will shoot first. Shooting a marble is like flipping a coin. Hold your shooter marble in your curled index finger, and tuck your thumb behind the marble. Flick the marble as hard as possible. Practice shooting the marble a few times away from the target marbles until it feels comfortable.
4. Most players kneel on the ground to shoot. You must "knuckle down" when you shoot. At least one knuckle of your shooting hand must be touching the ground until you have shot the marble. Lay your curled-up hand on the ground just outside of the circle with your knuckles down and thumb on top. Flick your shooter marble with your thumb toward the target marbles.
5. If you knock any target marbles out of the circle, set them beside you and shoot again. Knuckle down wherever your shooter marble stopped. If you did not knock any marbles out of the circle, pick up your shooter marble, and the next player shoots.
6. Continue to take turns shooting until all of the target marbles are cleared from the center ring. The player who knocked the most marbles out of the ring is the winner.

Spelling Bees and Examinations

Frontier schools invited the community to student activities and examinations. They spent the week decorating the interior of the school. Most students wore their best clothes to these activities.

Many frontier schools held spelling bees on Fridays or on an evening. Pioneer children learned to spell from *Noah Webster's Elementary Spelling Book* and *McGuffey's Speller*. The teacher used these textbooks during spelling bees. The teacher separated the class into two teams. Students from opposing teams took turns spelling words the teacher chose.

Students spelled each word dividing it into syllables. For example, to spell scarecrow, the student spelled s-c-a-r-e, then said 'scare.' Next, the student spelled c-r-o-w and said 'crow, scarecrow.' After each correctly spelled word, students went to the end of their team's line. If students misspelled their words, they returned to their seats. The spelling bee continued until only one student remained standing.

During the Christmas season, frontier schools often organized a pageant. This evening program combined songs, poetry readings, and academic drills into one event. A pageant often included a play. Students acted out familiar stories or wrote their own

Some pioneer schools held outdoor concerts and pageants. In 1899, these North Dakota students gathered in a wooded area for a music concert.

plays. The school invited the entire community to attend pageants.

Teachers tested the children's knowledge with end-of-term examinations. These exams quizzed the students on lessons they had learned throughout the year. Many teachers held public examinations to give the children a chance to show what they had learned. Students took pride in their work. Schoolchildren often recited poems and compositions. Some frontier teachers tested the students with oral exams. Teachers asked the student a question, and the student answered out loud.

During examinations, schoolteachers judged the students' progress. Children who performed well could move to the next grade.

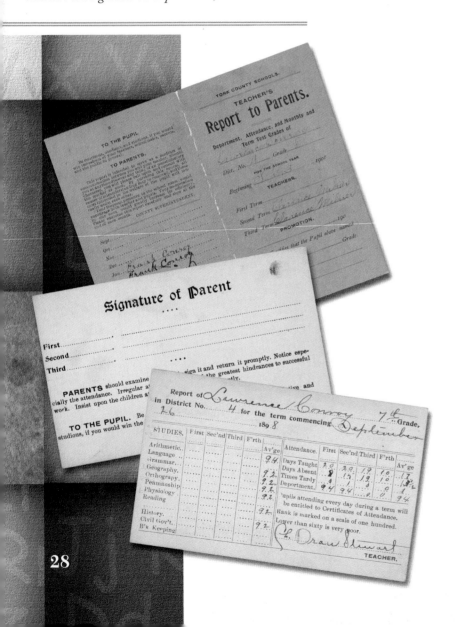

In order to graduate from school, older students had to pass a long oral test on a variety of topics. Students who passed this eighth-grade exam could advance to high school classes. But many students did not go to high school. Most students who did attend high school graduated when they were 15 or 16 years old. Teachers sometimes presented graduates with a decorated certificate.

After examinations, the pioneer community often gathered for a picnic. Frontier families brought food and played games at these community celebrations. At community picnics, pioneer families sometimes made ice cream or organized a taffy pull.

Many towns on the frontier continued to use one-room schoolhouses until the mid-1900s. As pioneer settlements grew, larger schools developed. People in frontier cities built public schools, academies, and colleges. These schools separated students according to grade level. By the early 1900s, most children attended school on a regular basis.

Have a Taffy Pull

What You Need

paper towel or napkin

measuring spoons

1½ tablespoons (22.5 mL) butter or
   margarine for greasing

baking pan, 8 inches by 8 inches
   (20 centimeters by 20 centimeters)

large saucepan

dry-ingredient measuring cups

liquid-ingredient measuring cup

1 cup (250 mL) sugar

1 tablespoon (15 mL) cornstarch

¾ cup (175 mL) light corn syrup

⅔ cup (150 mL) water

2 tablespoons (30 mL) butter or margarine

1 teaspoon (5 mL) salt

wooden spoon

candy thermometer

2 teaspoons (10 mL) vanilla

¼ teaspoon (1 mL) food coloring, optional

kitchen scissors

waxed paper or plastic wrap

What You Do

1. Use a paper towel or napkin dabbed with 1 tablespoon
   (22.5 mL) of butter to lightly grease the bottom and sides of
   the baking pan. Set pan aside.

2. In a saucepan, combine 1 cup (250 mL) sugar and 1 tablespoon
   (15 mL) cornstarch. Stir well.

3. Add ¾ cup (175 mL) light corn syrup, ⅔ cup (150 mL) water,
   2 tablespoons (30 mL) butter or margarine, and 1 teaspoon
   (5 mL) salt to the sugar mixture. Stir well.

4. Clip the candy thermometer to the side of the pan. Make sure
   the tip does not touch the bottom of the pan.

5. Over medium heat, stir the mixture constantly until it begins
   to boil. Stop stirring once the mixture begins to boil.

6. Continue to cook the mixture until the temperature on the
   thermometer reads 256°F (124°C), about 30 minutes.

7. Remove the saucepan from heat. Stir in 2 teaspoons (10 mL)
   of vanilla. Add ¼ teaspoon (1 mL) food coloring if desired.

8. Pour the mixture into baking pan and let cool.

9. When the candy is cool, use ½ tablespoon (7.5 mL) butter or
   margarine to lightly coat your fingers and the palms of
   your hands.

10. With a partner, pull and stretch the taffy until it looks light in
    color and becomes shiny and stiff.

11. Pull the taffy into strips about 6 inches (15 centimeters)
    wide. Use a kitchen scissors to cut the strips into
    bite-sized pieces.

12. Wrap the taffy pieces in waxed paper or plastic wrap
    to store.

Words to Know

board around (BORD uh-ROUND)—teachers' practice of moving between the homes of their students for meals and a room, offered as part of their salary

botany (BOT-uh-nee)—the science of studying plants

examination (eg-zam-uh-NAY-shuhn)—long spoken or written tests given to students at the end of the school term

frontier (fruhn-TEER)—the unsettled territories of western North America in the 1800s; the frontier stretched from the Missouri River to the California coast and included the upper midwestern states.

morals (MOR-uhls)—beliefs about what is right or wrong

normal school (NOR-muhl SKOOL)—a teacher's training college; normal training was offered in some high school classes.

philosophy (fuh-LOSS-uh-fee)—the study of wisdom, truth, and ideas

pioneer (pye-uh-NEER)—a person who settles in a new territory

prairie (PRAIR-ee)—a broad area of flat or rolling grassland with few or no trees

primer (PRIM-uhr)—a schoolbook used to teach children the alphabet and how to read

slate (SLAYT)—a gray rock that can be split into thin layers; pioneer students wrote on slates instead of paper.

sod (SOD)—a layer of soil with grass attached to it

sodbuster (SOD-buhst-uhr)—a plow used to break the soil for planting; also, a farmer who plowed up the sod layer of soil to plant a field sometimes was called a sodbuster.

switch (SWICH)—a long, thin stick that teachers sometimes used to whip students

To Learn More

Bial, Raymond. *One-Room School.* Boston: Houghton Mifflin, 1999.

Gillespie, Sarah. Edited by Suzanne L. Bunkers with Ann Hodgson. *A Pioneer Farm Girl: The Diary of Sarah Gillespie, 1877–1878.* Diaries, Letters, and Memoirs. Mankato, Minn.: Blue Earth Books, 2000.

O'Hara, Megan. *Pioneer Farm: Living on a Farm in the 1880s.* Living History. Mankato, Minn.: Blue Earth Books, 1998.

Patent, Dorothy Hinshaw. *Homesteading: Settling America's Heartland.* New York: Walker and Company, 1998.

Internet Sites

The American West
http://www.americanwest.com

Granville Village School
http://www.madriver.com/users/granschl/index.htm

Living History Farms
http://www.ioweb.com/lhf

The One-Room School Homepage
http://www.msc.cornell.edu/~weeds/SchoolPages/welcome.html

Pioneers Westward Expansion
http://www.kidinfo.com/American_History/Pioneers.html

Stuhr Museum of the Prairie Pioneer
http://www.stuhrmuseum.org

Places to Visit

Adams Schoolhouse
Westport Road
Easton, CT 06612

Conner Prairie
13400 Allisonville Road
Fishers, IN 46038

Pioneer Sholes School
Leroy Oakes Forest Preserve
Dean Street
St. Charles, IL 60174

Stuhr Museum of the Prairie Pioneer
3133 West Highway 34
Grand Island, NE 68801

Index